COMFORT *for* TROUBLED CHRISTIANS

J. C. Brumfield

MOODY PRESS
CHICAGO

God's children can be joyous and victorious even in the midst of the fire of trial and suffering.

In sickness and poverty, persecution and trial, abuse and betrayal, heartache and disappointment, God's child can have a perfect peace that passes all human understanding.

We dedicate this book to saints in affliction, with the humble prayer that His comfort might be a precious reality.

© 1961
MOODY BIBLE INSTITUTE

All Scripture quotations are from the King James Version.

ISBN: 0-8024-1426-5

1 3 5 7 9 10 8 6 4 2

Printed in the United States of America

COMFORT *for* TROUBLED CHRISTIANS

From the beginning of time, fire and water have been two of man's most essential needs. He cannot live without them, but they can be turned into his worst enemies.

In southern California recently a raging forest fire destroyed dozens of beautiful and expensive homes. As the people began to clear their property and make preparation for rebuilding, they became aware of a new danger—water. The priceless watershed had been destroyed, and with the coming of the winter rains a worse damage threatened than had caused the fire.

Is anything more dangerous than fire and water? In describing the trials of the saints, God uses these terms: "We went through fire and through water: but thou broughtest us out into a wealthy place" (Psalm 66:12). The word *wealthy* means abundant, a wide place, recovery, or refreshment. God describes the trials, troubles, and afflictions of His children as "fire and water" indicating that they are very severe. At first this would seem to be discouraging, but the joy, the victory, and the comfort are wrapped up in that word "through."

A Christian is never submerged in the flood and he is not consumed by the fire; he always passes "through." Even at the end of life the psalmist declared, "Though I walk through the valley of the shadow of death." These metaphors do not necessarily refer to different types of affliction, but teach the same truth regarding God's hand upon us. So we will consider the trial by fire.

God's Presence in Our Trial by Fire

Job compared his affliction to being cast into a "furnace." "When he hath tried me, I shall come forth as gold" (Job 23:10). Note the triumphant words "I shall come forth" ("through the fire"). It is one thing to testify after you have passed through the fire, but Job is still in the furnace. The heat is on, his boils shoot flashes of hot pain through his body, fever parches his lips, he scrapes his oozing boils with broken pieces of pottery. His head throbs with pain and his friends falsely accuse him, but he looks beyond his present fiery trial and shouts in vibrant, reassuring faith, "I shall come through."

Job saw himself "as gold" in the furnace. David saw the children of God "as silver" in the refiner's fire. "Thou hast tried us, as silver is tried" (Psalm 66:10). Malachi links both metals together in explaining divine chastening. "And he shall sit as a refiner and purifier of silver . . . and purge them as gold and silver" (Malachi 3:3). Why? Here is his answer, "that they may offer unto the Lord an offering in righteousness."

The divine method—"fire"

The divine motive—to "purge" and "purify"

The divine objective—our "righteousness"

There are five lessons we should and may learn from this refining and purging process.

He Cares

"He shall . . . purge them as gold and silver" (Malachi 3:3). Never let Satan inject a doubt into your mind regarding God's love for you. Satan would take advantage of your present trial and grief to whisper in your ear that "God doesn't care." But He does—you are so precious in His sight that nothing but the terms "gold and silver" can describe His concern. If "gold" and "silver" are precious to the refiner, how much more precious we must be to God. He paid a price far more than "silver and gold" for our redemption. It cost Him the blood of His only begotten Son. By comparison He refers to "silver and gold" as "corruptible." God gave all He had, the atoning blood of His precious Son to purchase our redemption.

What a comfort this should be! We are His most prized possessions, and He will allow nothing to harm us. That thing that happened to you is His means of increasing the value of His precious property. This is accomplished by increasing its beauty and purity. If we were worthless objects, we would never know the heat of the refiner's fire or the touch of His skillful hand. Beloved, the next time you feel the heat of a fiery trial, thank God. It is proof of your preciousness to Him. You are His blood-bought child, you belong to Him, you may be sure that He cares for His own.

He Cleanses

"He shall sit . . . and purge them" (Malachi 3:3). Every Christian who has ever been drawn near to the Lord knows something of the sinfulness of his heart and the impurity of his life. The closer we are to Him, the more conscious we become of our sinfulness and of our unworthiness.

Paul calls it the "flesh" (Romans 7) and "the body of this death." It is the self in our lives, the carnality, the unholiness, and it dogs our footsteps all along the Christian pathway. Chastening is a divine means of answering our prayer for cleansing. Did you not pray for God to cleanse you? He answered by putting you in the fire. He is cleansing as "a refiner and purifier of silver." The "dross" in your life is being burned in the fire of affliction.

Spend a moment in solemn reflection. What is the "dross" in your life that needs to be purged? It may be arrogance, pride, love of praise, love of attention, self-will, stubbornness, an unteachable spirit, peevishness, immaturity, jealousy, anger, impatience, love of money, selfishness, or an unforgiving spirit. All such "dross" grieves the Holy Spirit who dwells within us, and so we must be "refined" and "purged." This means we must pass "through the fire," but there's some comfort for you here. The refiner has a purpose—it is not to destroy his precious gold and silver, but to consume the "dross" and bring out the beauty and purity of the gold. Fire cannot destroy the gold; it only melts it. Oh, how we need to be melted before God! When the gold is melted, the dross floats on the top and it is easy for the refiner to skim it off. How long since you have been melted?

The three unyielding Hebrews were cast into Nebuchadnezzar's fiery furnace. It was seven times hotter than usual. Please note that they went into the furnace fully clothed and securely bound, but when they came out, three things were apparent. Not a hair of their heads was singed. More than that—the fire burned off their bands; and more wonderful still—the Lord had walked with them in the fire.

The same three things happen to the Christian in the fiery trial.

1. First, he is never harmed by the fire. Can you tell me that you were ever harmed by God's chastening? Oh, this doesn't mean that it doesn't hurt, but always the hurt is for our good.
2. Second, the fire sets him free from the shackles of carnality that hindered. The most radiant Christians are the ones who have suffered the most.
3. Third, God's presence is very real and precious in the fire.

The next time you feel the heat from the fire of affliction thank God that He is consuming not you, but the "dross" out of your life, and that you shall come *"through the fire"* purified and cleansed.

He Comforts

"And he shall sit as a refiner" (Malachi 3:3). This is a beautiful and comforting picture. The refiner never leaves his precious metal, but he sits by the fire and watches closely. He watches for that moment when the heat is sufficient to burn the dross and to leave the metal perfect. He knows just the right amount of heat to apply, and he applies it just the right length of time.

Have you ever felt like crying "I can't stand it" or

"It's more than I can bear"? No, my friend, it's not more than you can bear. Remember, "He sits by the fire"—He knows. So you *can* stand it. At a time like that, recall His promise in 1 Corinthians 10:13, "But God is faithful, [He sits by the fire] who will not suffer you to be tempted [tested] above that ye are able; but will with the temptation [trial] also make a way to escape, that *ye may be able to bear it*." So you *can* bear it. Never forget His promise "my grace *is* sufficient for thee" (2 Corinthians 12:9).

I have gained help and inspiration in the preparation of this Bible study from David Kirk's book, *The Mystery of Divine Chastening*. He tells the story of two Christian martyrs during the Reformation. One was a veteran saint, Latimer, and the other was a young believer, Riley. They were condemned to be burned at the stake. The night before the execution young Riley was highly nervous and very agitated. He looked through the iron bars of their dungeon prison and saw the people preparing the stakes. In his panic he tried to light a candle and in the process burned his finger. His burn impressed upon him the greater agony of the fate that awaited him and he cried out, "I can't stand it, I can't stand it." His seasoned companion gently laid his hand upon his shoulder and said, "My friend, God didn't ask you to burn your finger, so He doesn't give grace to stand it tonight, but tomorrow, when the time comes, God will give sufficient grace." The next morning the two men were led to the stakes, each with a triumphant smile and perfect peace in his heart. As the flames surrounded their bodies, out of the midst came their vibrant voices united in a victorious song of praise. Yes, my friend, God gives grace for everything He calls upon you to bear.

I read some time ago about a train that was traveling through the night in a violent storm. The lightning flashed, the rain splattered in windy gusts against the windows. The water was rising along the tracks and the passengers were seized with terror. In the midst of the confusion one little girl seemed to be in perfect peace. Her unusual calm at such a time of excitement amazed the passengers. Finally one man asked, "How is it that you can be so calm when all the rest of us are so worried?" She smiled sweetly and said, "My father is the engineer."

Why not bow your head right now and thank God that your heavenly Father has His hand upon the throttle? The fire is controlled. He will not send more than you can bear, but with every temptation will provide a way of escape.

He Controls

"And He shall sit . . . and purge them as gold and silver" (Malachi 3:3).

In our former picture of the refiner sitting by the fire, we focused our attention on the fact that *he is controlling the fire.* Now I would emphasize the fact that *he* sits by the fire *to guard, protect, and care for his precious metal.* Fix your eyes upon the One who controls the fire. He's there. "When thou passest through the waters, I will be with thee" (Isaiah 43:2). No beloved, God never throws His precious ones into the flames and forgets that they are there—He "sits by the fire"—"I will be with thee."

The aged apostle Paul was in the dungeon. He knew that his life was soon to end. Many friends had deserted him. The loyalty of others was questionable, but there was a note of victory in his last letter to young Timothy. "Notwithstanding the Lord stood with me, and strengthened me" (2 Timothy 4:17).

Are you experiencing the test of fire and affliction? Thank God that He is there. He sits by the fire. He is there to comfort, to strengthen, and to encourage. Reach out by faith and take His hand. Look up into His face and let His presence reassure you.

He Knows

"And he shall sit as a refiner and purifier of silver" (Malachi 3:3).

You see, He knows when the work is done. Here we have the key to the entire finishing process. Sometimes we might think the fire too long, that instead of purifying it will destroy. You say, "How does the refiner know when the fire has done its perfect work?"

An old refiner was asked that question by a visitor. He answered, "See how I sit by the fire?" The stranger answered, "Yes." Then he said, "See how I bend over the pot?" Again the stranger said, "Yes, but how do you know when there has been just the right amount of heat?" The old refiner looked up and said, *"When I see my own reflection."*

God's purpose in creation is revealed in Genesis 1:26, "Let us make man in *our image.*" But the image was terribly defaced and marred by sin, so God redeemed us by the precious blood of Christ. It is only in one in whom the Spirit of God dwells that the image and likeness of God may be reflected. This is God's great and eternal purpose for His children, "to be conformed to the image of his Son" (Romans 8:29). "And as we have borne the image of the earthy, we shall also bear the image of the heavenly" (1 Corinthians 15:49). God's will is that every Christian might be "conformed to the image of his Son." This is a process in the life of every believer. "But we all . . . beholding as in a glass the glory of the Lord, are changed into the same image from glory to glory even as by the Spirit of the Lord" (2 Corinthians 3:18).

Chastening is God's means to this end. The Christlike life cannot be produced apart from suffering. If you want to bear His image, never shrink from the refiner's fire. I fear that we often want the results without paying the price. Paul knew the price. He said, "That I may know him, and the power of his resurrection, and the fellowship of his sufferings, being made conformable unto his death" (Philippians 3:10).

Are you sick and discouraged, weak and weary, facing trials and troubles that seem more than you can bear? Then remember these five glorious facts.

HE CARES—You are precious to Him "as silver and gold."

HE CLEANSES—The fire purifies "and purge[s] them."

HE CONTROLS—Yes, the fire is under control. "He shall sit as a refiner."

HE COMFORTS—He's with you in the fire. "And he shall sit" by the fire.

HE KNOWS—Be assured He know when the work is done. He looks for His image. Climb upon the pinnacle of faith with Job and cry, "When he hath tried me, I shall come forth as gold" (Job 23:10).

The Cure for Worry

"Be careful for nothing; but in every thing by prayer and supplication with thanksgiving let your requests be made know unto God. And the peace of God, which passeth all understanding, shall keep your hearts and minds through Christ Jesus" (Philippians 4:6–7).

I never knew my father to worry. He had a serenity of faith, a completeness of surrender, a submission to God's will, and a freedom from selfish ambition that I have not witnessed in any other Christian.

I saw him betrayed by friends he trusted, falsely accused by enemies of the Gospel, disappointed in the wrecking of plans that were conceived through months of prayer, and crushed by circumstances he did not create, but I never knew my father to fret and worry.

I saw his heart broken, his ministry hindered, and his family suffer, but I never saw him lose his deep, abiding inner calmness and sweetness of spirit. Most Christians know so little of such complete victory in Christ that they are inclined to misinterpret it for weakness or unconcern.

But this freedom from anxious care is the promise of God's Word, and I believe it is possible for every Christian to attain.

"Be careful [anxious] for nothing; but in every thing by prayer and supplication with thanksgiving let your requests be made known unto God. And the peace of God, which passeth all understanding, shall keep your hearts and minds through Christ Jesus" (Philippians 4:6–7).

It is easy to say no Christian should worry, but it is hard to put into actual practice. To scold and condemn does not help. The one who worries is the one who is most anxious not to worry and is the most hurt by it and unhappy about it. I want to help—not rebuke.

"But how," you say, "can a Christian avoid worry and possess a calm and confident spirit that bears testimony to the sufficiency of God's grace?"

I do not possess any magic formula and I do not profess to have attained the ultimate in this regard myself, but whatever degree of success I may have reached I owe to the simple formula outlined in God's Word.

Let us have a look at worry—the disease—the cure—and the consequences.

The Disease

❖

WORRY IS A DISEASE

Worry is now recognized by physicians as a disease (sometimes even a contagious disease). Dr. James W. Barton said recently, "It is known that about one half of the patients consulting a physician have no organic disease. In about one-fourth of the cases, the cause of the symptoms is tenseness or worry, strain, and fatigue . . . prolonged shock or fear [which is really worry] can affect the workings of all the organs of the body."

Dr. Alverez (formerly of Mayo Clinic) said, "Worry is the cause of most stomach trouble."

Dr. Han Selye, writing about the stress theory of disease, said, "Stress is the trigger which causes disease."

Dr. Emerson, an outstanding Christian psychologist, stated there are five underlying causes of mental illness and frustration (often caused by worry, and often the cause of physical illness): fear, hate, guilt, inferiority, and insecurity.

These may be analyzed as follows:

1. A supersensitivity to criticism
2. An excessive awareness of our weaknesses
3. An abnormal pride of our achievements
4. An unobtainable ambition beyond our abilities
5. An absorbing jealousy over the success of others
6. A sinful covetousness of things beyond our reach (or financial means).

❖

WORRY IS A SIN

God says, "Be [anxious] for nothing" (Philippians 4:6). This is a clear command and to break God's commandment is sin. A healthy person may be transformed into an invalid in a few months by worry. Clinical case histories in the offices of physicians and institutions all over the world bear ample proof of this.

How about our spiritual lives? Worry chokes the Word of God and keeps our lives from being fruitful.

"And some fell among thorns; and the thorns sprung up, and choked them. . . . He also that received seed among the thorns is he that heareth the word; and the care of this world . . . choke the word, and he becometh unfruitful" (Matthew 13:7, 22).

❖

WORRY IS UNNECESSARY

God does not expect the impossible of us. He

clearly commands in Philippians 4:6, "Be careful [anxious] for nothing." "Stop being worried about anything" (Williams translation). "Do not fret or have anxiety" (Amplified). "Entertain no worry" (Berkeley).

Not only is worry a sin and a disease, but it becomes foolish because it is not necessary. I would not ridicule our worries because they are real. That's what makes them so dangerous, but it is foolish to carry our worries instead of placing them upon the Lord. "Casting all your care upon him; for he careth for you" (1 Peter 5:7). Just to have someone to care is often the first step in the cure of worry. "God shall supply all your need" (Philippians 4:19).

Someone said, "Today is the tomorrow you worried about yesterday."

A woman in Korea was given a peck of rice by her mother-in-law. She started home and put the rice on the floor of a conveyance that was pulled by a servant. As she sat down she thought, "This rice in addition to my own weight might be too heavy." So she placed the rice on her head and kept it there all the way.

We are just as foolish when we carry our worries instead of placing them on the Lord. What is the matter? Do we think God is not big enough?

"Be [anxious] for nothing." "Cast thy burden upon the Lord" (Psalm 55:22). "God shall supply all your need." In these quotations God gets to the basic cause of our frustrations: worries, anxieties, and fears.

Let us just be honest and admit that we do not trust God completely—we do not leave everything in His hands.

Dr. Bob Cook recently said, "You never need lift a finger to defend yourself unless you are not quite sure that God can handle the matter." Our worries indicate that we just do not think God is big enough to handle the problem without our help. Such worry dishonors the Lord, belittles our God, and doubts His Word.

❖

Said the Robin to the Sparrow,
"I would really like to know
Why these anxious human beings
Rush about and worry so."
Said the Sparrow to the Robin,
"Friend, I think that it must be
That they have no heavenly Father
Such as cares for you and me."
—Elizabeth Cheney, 1859

❖

The Cure

First of all, a doctor cannot cure the disease of worry. His pills doctor the symptoms and not the cause.

He can give tranquilizers and keep people from "exploding," but when the effect of the pill wears off the tensions remain. The basic cause remains.

He can give us sleeping pills and help us forget for a few hours, but when we awake, the problem is still there.

A psychiatrist cannot cure worry. If he is honest, he is the first to admit this. He can probe into our subconscious mind and dig out the reason, but when he finds it he does not know what to do with it (unless he is a Christian).

Now if the doctor cannot cure it and a psychiatrist cannot cure it, then is there any cure? Yes! *The Christian has within him a supernatural life.* A life of worry is on the *natural* plane. The Christian life is on a *spiritual* plane.

The believer is exhorted to "be careful for nothing," but God does not stop at that. He tells us how to get rid of cares: "By prayer and supplication with thanksgiving let your requests be made known unto God. And the peace of God, which passeth all understanding, shall keep your hearts and minds through Christ Jesus" (Philippians 4:6–7).

God's formula cures all three symptoms: mental, physical, and spiritual.

No one without the "peace of God" can possibly get rid of his fears, anxieties, tensions, frustrations, and worries. The peace of God is not secured through the doctor's prescription or the psychiatrist's couch. The cure is prescribed in the Word of God.

❖

BY PRAYER

"In every thing by prayer" (Philippians 4:6). Someone recently said, "Seven days without prayer makes one weak."

You have no worry that you cannot take to God in prayer. You come to God not as a beggar, but as His child.

"Cast thy burden upon the Lord." How do you do that? You talk to Him about it—that's prayer—put the burden on Him, and leave it there. The first step the psychiatrist uses is "talk it out." We have Someone better to whom to talk.

Suppose two planks are laid across the stream, but one is sound and the other is rotten. Now if you attempt to walk on both the planks, you will certainly get wet because the rotten one will break.

"Casting all your care upon him; for he careth for you" (1 Peter 5:7). Do not bring out your rotten plank and try to help. That is why you fall. That is why you wet your pillow with tears. Cast "*all* your care upon him." When you have cast it there, trust God. He is big enough. He does not need your help.

❖

BY PRAISE

"In every thing by prayer" (Philippians 4:6). Note the words "every thing." The small affairs of life as well as the big and important. It is by attempting to handle the little things ourselves that we get into trouble. Nothing that troubles us is too trifling to bring to God—that is the way to "pray without ceasing." We need to learn to praise God for *every thing* and to pray to Him about *every thing.*

❖

"WITH THANKSGIVING"

"In every thing by prayer and supplication with *thanksgiving*" (Philippians 4:6).

"With thanksgiving let your requests be made known unto God." We need to thank God for past mercies. The memory of them will give us confidence.

God appeared to Moses in Moses' moment of weakness and fear. God calmed his heart with these words, "I am the Lord thy God, which have brought thee out of the land of Egypt, out of the house of bondage" (Exodus 20:2). Moses recalled the mighty wisdom and power of God as He led that great host of people out of bondage and slavery. He was reassured.

"In every thing . . . with thanksgiving" . . . because "all things work together for good" . . . because you can be assured that "this is the will of God . . . concerning you" (1 Thessalonians 5:18). It is easy to trust God when there is no trouble, but it is more needful when trouble comes.

My friend, are you living a life of prayer, praise, and thanksgiving? It is a very simple cure, it is good medicine, it has a sweet flavor, and it never fails.

Go somewhere alone with God and take God's cure. First by prayer—talk to Him about it. "Let your requests be made known unto God" (Philippians 4:6).

Next try praising. Think of all the little everyday blessing that you take for granted and never even stop to thank Him for. This will naturally lead to the third step, "with thanksgiving." Spend some time thanking God for all of the blessings He has given you in the past and has showered upon you now.

The Consequences

"The peace of God, which passeth all understanding, shall keep your hearts and minds through Christ Jesus" (Philippians 4:7).

This is the sure result of taking God's cure for worry.

There may be no change in the circumstances, but there will come a great change in your heart and mind.

Paul prayed three times for his "thorn in the flesh" to be removed. God's answer came back each time, "My grace is sufficient for thee" (2 Corinthians 12:9). The *conditions* were not changed, but his *heart* was changed and his *attitude* toward his affliction was changed because of the reassuring Word of God.

Now what is the result (or consequences) of God's cure for worry?

❖

THE PEACE OF GOD

"The peace of God . . . shall keep your hearts and minds" (Philippians 4:7).

Peace with God was secured at Calvary through faith in Jesus Christ. The peace of God floods the soul when we pray, praise, and thank Him.

That is the way! God promises, "The peace of God . . . shall keep your hearts and minds." That is the secret of having peace—the peace of God in our *minds* and *hearts.* Take your burdens to the Lord and *leave* them there.

Many who have peace with God know little of the peace of God. It's *God's own peace,* which He imparts and implants, and which calms our mind.

We cannot think of God ever being anxious or worried or disturbed, can we?

No, He is omnipotent, all-powerful; nothing is too big for Him.

He is omniscient, all-knowing; nothing can take Him by surprise.

He is omnipresent; He is everywhere.

Now since that is true, can we not trust Him? And if we trust Him, can we not have *His peace* in our hearts?

To say the least, worry is doubting God. "Take no thought, saying, What shall we eat? or, What shall we drink? or, Wherewithall shall we be clothed? (For after all these things do the Gentiles seek:) for your heavenly Father knoweth that ye have need of all these things" (Matthew 6:31–32).

❖

WHICH PASSES UNDERSTANDING

"The peace of God, which passeth all understanding" (Philippians 4:7).

That's the peace—the kind of perfect peace that God has and that He will give to us! A peace that is so wonderful, you will be surprised when you find you possess it. A peace that is so strange "under the circumstances," that you cannot understand how you have it—it passes understanding.

"Thou wilt keep him in *perfect peace,* whose mind is stayed on thee" (Isaiah 26:3). When we keep our minds fixed on Christ, His greatness, His power, His love, then He keeps our minds in perfect peace, a peace past all human understanding.

❖

THROUGH CHRIST JESUS

This is why a psychiatrist cannot cure and a doctor's pills give only temporary relief. There is no cure for worry aside from the Lord Jesus Christ!

Outside the Lord Jesus Christ I can offer you no hope, no cure for worry, no relief from your anxiety, and no lasting help from your trouble. Let us look again at the five basic causes of mental illness, frustrations, and worry.

1. **Fear.** This is an increasing problem with physicians, but it only fulfills the prophecy in God's Word concerning the last days, "men's hearts failing them for fear." There is no cure for fear outside of the Lord, but God will "keep them in perfect peace" who trust Him.

2. **Hate.** The cure for hate is love, and God is love. You do not get love in pills at a drugstore. Many people have been made desperately ill by hate.

3. **Guilt.** The psychiatrist may expose a guilt complex, but he cannot do anything about it. God's promise is, "If we confess our sins, he is faithful and just to forgive us our sins, and to cleanse us from all unrighteousness" (1 John 1:9). Only the blood of Jesus Christ can remove the feeling of guilt. Only the assurance of God's forgiveness can relieve a troubled mind.

4. **Inferiority.** It is more than a bolstered ego that we need. We must have a sense of "belonging." What better cure is there than to belong to the family of God?

5. **Insecurity.** A savings account in the bank or the mortgage paid off on the home will not purchase freedom from worry. Some of the most wealthy people are the most worried. Real security can only be found in the assurance of eternal life and it is *"through Christ Jesus."* A troubled heart is the result of unbelief. "Let not your heart be troubled: ye believe in God, believe also in me" (John 14:1).

What to Do with Your Troubles

If you have some troubles, cheer up—God is keeping His promise. "In the world ye shall have tribulation" (John 16:33).

He does not promise us a life without problems, sorrow, or trials, but He does tell us what to do with them. Jesus said, "be of good cheer; I have overcome the world."

Paul was in trouble; he was a prisoner on the way to Rome in a creaky old ship. He faced trial by Caesar, who was not noted for friendship with the Christians. The "contrary winds," a storm, shipwreck, and "no hope." Have you ever been at the place of "no hope"? Do you know what Paul did? He said "I believe God." Do you really *believe* Him? Really?

It is not only the words we speak, but the circumstances under which we say them that reveal real character. "I believe God" is easy to say, but no one ever said it under more unbelievable circumstances than Paul. The story is recorded in Acts 27, and it gives us one of the great pictures of faith in the Bible.

We may liken Paul's voyage to life. It is truly a "voyage of faith." I pray that this Bible study will give you some help in your own voyage of life.

Get Started

"We launched" (Acts 27:2). Paul's consuming passion for years had been to preach the gospel in

Rome. Under the providence of God, he was arrested, tried and convicted, and appealed to Caesar. When Agrippa examined Paul he might have set him free if he had not appealed to Caesar.

It was not a mistake—Paul was on his way to Rome with Caesar paying the fare. The centurion, Julius, was given charge of the prisoners.

"We launched" meant that they committed themselves unto the sea. First, "It was determined that we should sail" (verse 1). They made up their minds to go, then started. They would not have arrived in Rome if they had not "launched." Dreams, visions, desires, and resolutions have their place, but what we need is faith to launch.

Some people never accomplish anything because they never start. Others are so afraid of making a mistake they never do anything. I would rather do something the wrong way than do nothing; I could at least learn something from the mistake.

There are thousands of Christians who honestly desire to do something for Christ, but they never accomplish it because they never get started. Good intentions are not enough. Begin—launch—start!

Don't Stop

"The winds were contrary" (Acts 27:4).

Notice the progress of the story, "exceedingly tossed with a tempest" (verse 18), "neither sun nor stars" appeared (verse 20), and "all hope that we should be saved was then taken away." *That's where faith begins.*

Notice the order! "We launched"—"the winds were contrary." Start something for the Lord and the devil will stir up a contrary wind. The Christian life is not always smooth sailing; storms arise, winds blow, Satan opposes. If you start something for God, the devil will send a storm.

Paul had been talking to God about their predicament. Hidden away somewhere in the lower part of the ship, Paul prayed. It pays to be on praying terms with God when trouble comes. Some people never pray until too late. Then they cannot get anywhere.

Jonah did not pray until he found himself in the belly of the fish. Then he started to pray, but he was not on praying terms. He was cold, backsliden, and stubborn, and it took a disaster to get him to pray. If Jonah had been on praying terms when the old whale opened his mouth to swallow him, Jonah could have called "God, help me," and the fish would have had to give him up. If backsliding, rebelling, and resisting God cost nothing else but the privilege of prayer, it is a terrible price to pay.

Believe God

"I believe God" (Acts 27:25).

It's easy to get up in a prayer meeting and say, "I believe God." It takes a real faith to say it when a storm is raging. Get on the boat with Paul and say it; get at the place of "no hope" and say it.

The experienced sailors said, "No hope." "All hope that we should be saved was taken away" (27:20). They had exhausted the skill of experienced seamen and the verdict was "no hope." The soldiers said, "No hope," and were going to kill the prisoners, but the centurion stopped them. The circumstances indicated "no hope." The jagged lightning seemed to spell out the words in the black sky—"no hope." The howling wind added its voice to the wailing chorus, "no hope." The flapping sails, plunging waves, creaking ship, and cracking masts all seemed to echo the fatal cry, "no hope."

Reason argued like this—the storm is too great, the ship is too small, the load is too heavy, and the distance is too great—"no hope." Have you ever been at the place of no hope? You will never know the greatness of God until you stand there. Maybe you *are* at the place of "no hope," and if so, take courage. There is a way out.

For many years my wife experienced poor health. Some specialists on the West Coast made an unsuccessful surgical attempt and said, "There's no hope."

Mayo Clinic was in our minds a "court of last resort." I wrote to them that I was bringing her there. I made some quick changes in my car and installed a full-length bed. Then, with the baby and a full tank of oxygen, we started out. When I arrived there was a letter waiting for us. "Your wife's condition is a huge balloon cyst of the lung, filling entire right thorax. The condition has progressed until frequent decompressions are necessary. When this stage is reached there is nothing that can be done and the patient dies." That was written more than ten years ago and she is in good health today. The Lord had to bring us to the place of "no hope" before we really knew what it was to trust Him. He miraculously kept her alive until new surgical techniques were developed. When we get to the place of "no hope," God just begins to work.

God spoke to Paul, saying, "Fear not, Paul; thou must be brought before Caesar" (27:24). And Paul said, *"I believe God."* Here doubtless he challenged the elements: "Do your worst, winds, waves, and rolling sea; blow your hardest, Euroclydon; hide your face, sun and moon and stars; give up if you will, soldiers and sailors, but *I believe God!"*

He did not believe the experts, he did not believe the soldiers, he did not believe the dictates of common sense—he believed God. Sometimes the "experts" are wrong, sometimes soldiers make mistakes, and sometimes faith does not seem to act in accordance with common sense, but God never fails.

God spoke. How like God to speak a word of comfort at a time like that! How did God speak? I believe He spoke to Paul through the angel in an audible voice, but He doesn't speak that way now. We are under the dispensation of grace. He speaks by the prompting of the Holy Spirit, by the "still small voice" within. He speaks through open and closed doors. He speaks through His Word. It pays to hide God's Word in the heart for such a time.

"I believe God" spoken at a time like that gives us one of the great pictures of faith in the Bible. I wish I could paint it on canvas, the ship tossing on the crest of the waves like an eggshell, waves plunging over the deck, Paul clinging to the rigging of the ship, drenched with angry water and splashed by hungry waves! Ocean spray must have stung his weathered face, but he lifted his head in victory as he shouted above the roar of the storm, "I believe God."

Man was helpless in the face of the storm, but God had made a promise to Paul, and Paul believed Him. Paul had a choice—to fear the storm or to believe God.

Maybe you are in a similar place. A storm rages, clouds are dark, threatening thunder rolls, enemies oppose, and circumstances overwhelm you. Advisers cry, "no hope," but above the confusion God *speaks,* "When thou passest through the waters, I will be with thee . . . they shall not overflow thee" (Isaiah 43:2). You have a choice to stand on the promise of His Word or to believe circumstances. God has a promise for every trial, test, need, temptation, and circumstance of life. Faith chooses to believe God.

It pays to believe God, not only for ourselves but for others. On that ship were 276 others—saved because Paul was on board. The angel said, "God hath given thee all them that sail with thee" (v. 24). Paul must have prayed for them—the angel said, "God hath given thee." Paul thought of the others as well as of himself.

Believe God. *Believe God!* He has Something To Say To You—Are You Listening?

It Is So Simple

"I believe" (Acts 27:25).

Here we delight in divine simplicity.

It means, I may not understand it, I do not deserve it, I cannot explain it, but I believe it. It is a simple formula. God said it—I believe it. That is faith.

A man was noted for great faith. A preacher looked him up and asked, "Are you the man with great faith?" He said, "No, I'm the man with a very little faith in a great God." God wants us to believe when we cannot see, cannot understand, and cannot explain. If we could see and understand, it would not be faith.

It is not so much the *amount* of faith as the *object* of your faith that counts. Not *what* you believe, but *whom* you believe. The sailors trusted their ability. The soldiers trusted the sailors. The captain trusted the pilot. The pilot trusted his compass. They all trusted the ship. The ship relied on the anchor, and the anchor failed. Paul trusted God and God never fails. It is easy to believe when the waters are smooth, but it takes real faith to trust when the storm comes.

In the very next chapter of Acts we learn they were on shore. The men were building a fire when a deadly snake came out of a bundle of sticks and fastened itself on Paul's hand. The natives were certain that it was sure death. Paul had no fear. He calmly shook it into the fire. Why was he not afraid? He believed God. God had promised, "Thou must be brought before Caesar" (v. 24). Paul believed Him.

You Belong

"Whose I am" (Acts 27:23).

Here we have a confession of divine ownership.

It must have sounded strange to those idol worshiping sailors who owned their gods to hear Paul say, "My God owns me." The shipping company owned the vessel, the captain owned the sailors, the government owned the soldiers, and the soldiers owned the prisoners, but God owned Paul! Stop! Think! God owns you. "Ye are not your own . . . ye are bought with a price" (1 Corinthians 6:19–20).

A little girl heard a missionary challenge at church and she wanted to give. Thinking of her newest possession, she said, "I'll give my new dress to Jesus." The pastor explained that God could not use her gift. Then she offered to give her doll, but the pastor again explained that God could not use it. Then she stepped into the offering plate when it was passed and said, "I'll give myself to Jesus." That's what God wants.

❖

You Belong. You Belong to Him.
Are You Not Glad? Then Tell Him So.

❖

Do You Serve?

"Whom I serve" (Acts 27:23).

Here is demonstrated proper obedience.

This must have sounded strange to the sailors. Their heathen gods served them, and they would get them out of the sailor chest in time of storm. The vessel served the company, the sailors served the captain, the soldiers served the government, and the prisoners served the soldiers, but Paul served God. "There stood by me this night . . . whose I am . . . and whom I serve" (v. 23). Sometimes we are blind to the opportunity to witness for Christ, but Paul went out of his way to give this bold confession. Paul bore the marks of divine ownership in his body, marks made by the Romans. He had been beaten three times; he bore the red angry scars of those stripes that had been laid on him in the synagogue. He bore the ugly scars left by the cruel stones that had beaten him down until he was left for dead. No wonder Paul said, "I bear in my body the marks of the Lord Jesus" (Galatians 6:17). They were proof as to whom he belonged and whom he served. It cost Paul something to belong to Christ and to serve Him. How much has it ever cost you to serve Christ? If you are paying a price now don't complain—"count it all joy" (James 1:2).

He Stands By

"There stood by me this night the angel of God" (Acts 27:23).

Here we see divine faithfulness.

What night? The night of the storm, the night of despair, the night of "no hope." How like God to stand by at such a time! He who has never been in a storm on the sea of life has never known the sweetness of God's presence. God has promised that He will give His angels "charge over thee" (Luke 4:10)—"I will never leave thee, nor forsake thee" (Hebrews 13:5)—"I will be with [thee] in trouble" (Psalm 91:15). If we suffer, we don't suffer alone.

❖

"Just when I need Him, Jesus is near.
Just when I falter, just when I fear.
Ready to help me, ready to cheer.
Just when I need Him most."
—W. C. Poole

❖

Does it seem like you have been forsaken? No one understands, no one cares? Take courage, when all others fail, God will stand by. He stood by Paul, saying, "Fear not."

You Will Make It

"They escaped all safe" (Acts 27:44).

Here is divine deliverance.

The ship finally crashed on the rocks and broke in pieces. Some people could swim; others got ashore on pieces of wreckage. Note, the ship had to be broken up before they could get to shore on broken pieces. So God sometimes has to take every human means of deliverance away from us before He can undertake. God promised Paul that all with him would be saved. God always keeps His promise.

Trust Him. Commit your life to the Lord Jesus Christ. Storms may come, winds may blow, enemies may attack, Satan may oppose, circumstances may seem impossible, but He has said, "I'll stand by you." "I'll never leave or forsake you." "You shall never perish." God doesn't promise an easy life. He said, "In the world ye shall have tribulation" (John 16:33). Tribulations cannot overcome us. Trials cannot crush us. Enemies cannot destroy us. Sickness cannot defeat us. Temptation cannot cripple us and all hell cannot destroy us. God's ultimate triumph has already been recorded in His unchanging Word—"all safe" at last. Take courage, look up, "believe God," and thank Him for the victory.

"I believe God."

All Things Work Together for Good

"And we know that all things work together for good to them that love God, to them who are the called according to his purpose" (Romans 8:28).

Then quit trembling and trust. Quit pouting and praise. Quit running and rest. Quit worrying and wait. Quit belittling and believe!

But!—mystery engulfs, enemies assail, friends desert, Satan buffets, demons beset, sins infest, sickness weakens, sorrows distress, death robs, and poverty threatens; air castles crumble, dreams vanish in the air, ships go on the reef, raging storms sweep down, and dark clouds of perplexity swallow you up. But why? Why? Why? *Life has, to many, become one great question mark.* The world today crawls out from under the wreckage of a tottering civilization and writes a giant question mark across the rolling black clouds of mystery and confusion. WHY? WHY? WHY? Has God deserted you? Has His promise failed you? Has Jesus forgotten you? Has the Holy Spirit deserted you? No, troubled friend. God has answered the believer. "All things work together for good" and

❖

God is still on the throne,
He ever cares for His own.
His promise is true;

37

He will not forget you,
God is still on the throne.

❖

His promises bind Him to help you, His compassion inclines Him to hear you, and His power enables Him to deliver you. Be grateful for what He has done. Thank Him for what He is doing. Trust Him for what He will do. Quit asking "why" and praise him that Romans 8:28 is still in "the Book."

This is one of the most blessed promises God has given us, yet one of the most doubted and misunderstood. You are not required to understand it, but to believe it, to act upon it, and to make it a working principle in your life. This is the promise of God, and the child of God can, through faith, turn God's promise into a prophecy. "I do not know what tomorrow holds, but I do know that it will all 'work for good.'"

The Promise—Not for Everybody

I would point out to you that this is a *narrow* promise.

It does not say, "All things work together for good *for all people*," but rather "to them that love God, to them who are *the called*" (Romans 8:28). It is clear that this is a promise to the child of God, one who has, through faith in Christ, been born again. To the child of God it is certainly true, "God, that cannot lie, promised" (Titus 1:2). Praise God it is true.

Circumstances in your life cannot alter the sure promise of God. You can stand by the casket containing the remains of the dearest one on earth, and these words are as true as the heavenly Father who spoke them. In the hour of your deepest sorrow, hardest trial, and greatest disappointment, in the moment of testing, sifting, and temptation, as in your greatest joys and victories, it is true, "all things work together for good." Remember, friend, that what you face today does not change the eternal Word of God. Let us notice exactly what God has promised, and I believe that through His Spirit we can come to *understand* it as well as to *believe* it.

We Know

"We know." What blessed assurance! Not we understand, or enjoy, or can see, or can feel, but *"we know." We know* because God has said it and our personal experience confirms it. Thank God that we can know. We can only *hope* for the things that are temporal and material in this world, but the eternal and precious things we can know. For example, we may lay up treasures on earth and hope that they are safe; yet we may lose everything that we have; but we can lay up treasures in heaven and *know* that they are not where "moth and rust doth corrupt, and where thieves break through and steal" (Matthew 6:19).

We are alive today, and *hope* to be tomorrow, but if we know Christ as our Saviour, we have *eternal* life and know that we have "passed from death unto life" (1 John 3:14). We may be faring well in life today and *hope* for continued blessings tomorrow; yet before the rising of another sun, our hearts may be broken, our health gone, our dreams shattered, and our loved ones taken from us. But if we are God's children, we can "*know* that all things work together for good."

All Things

"All things," not some things, most things, the pleasant things, or the easy things, but "all things." We usually have no difficulty in seeing this truth when all is going well for us, but it includes the hard, bitter, testing things of life as well—"all things," from the most minute to the most momentous, from the humblest event in daily providence to the crisis hours in grace—"all things work together for good."

The fact is that the hardest things to bear have in reality been the *best* for us. *No sorrow leaves us where it found us; it either drives us from God or brings us near to Him.* For example, the remorse of Judas drove him to suicide, but the remorse of Peter transformed the impulsive disciple into "the rock." Look upon every time of sorrow and trouble as a turning point in your Christian life. You will come out of it either closer to the Lord or farther from Him.

God does not promise that our lives shall always be pleasant, but He does declare that even the unpleasant things are a part of His "all things." He does not promise material prosperity at all times, but even the *need* we have shall "work together for good." Some of the greatest spiritual blessings that have ever come into our lives are times when we have had to literally pray, "Give us this day our daily bread" (Matthew 6:11). Some of us complain because we are in poor health, but many of the greatest spiritual victories we have ever won have been in times when God has laid us aside a while to commune with Him and to learn the rich lessons He has for us on "the bed of affliction."

God Is Working

"All things work." Notice it is in the present tense. They are working, not have worked, shall work, should work, or might work, but "all things work." We complain so often, "I can't see the results," but that is no sign that God is not working. I fear that we are too much inclined to measure things according to what we see. Where is the Christian who has not had some dark experience in his life that he could not for the moment understand? The black clouds of mystery engulf him, a thousand demons seem to surround him, the face of God seems to be hidden—there seems to be no way out. Then in the darkness of the hour he cries, "It can't be true—I am at a standstill in life. I'm not getting anywhere. No good could come from this." Then the sun rises on the other side of that black night and he looks back on the experience and sees the loving hand of God through it all. "All things *work*." In fact, the hardest things are often the best things for us. The morning just reveals what God had been doing in the night. Are you today at a place in life where it all seems dark? Take hold of this blessed promise. Can't you trust Him in the dark? You do not have to see to know that God is working on your behalf. The sun will rise in the morning; the black clouds will roll away. Then you will see that God is working on your behalf *today.*

"Together"

"All things work together," not separately or independently, not each thing in itself, but "together." This is the key to the test. God does not promise all things work for good, or each thing is good in itself, but "all things work *together* for good." Many people pick out one experience in life and wave it in the face of God and challenge, "I don't see any good in that." No, and God doesn't say there is, but it is a part of the "all things," a part of the divine pattern. The separate events of life may seem to be disastrous, but "together" they "work for good." It takes a blending of the experiences in life to make the "together." When we are living in submission and obedience to

His will, every event has a definite place in the plan and pattern of God. Each thing is a part of the "all things," and "all things together work for good." Sugar is sweet to the taste and adds flavor to much of our food. However, you would not want to make a meal of sugar alone. Nothing would be more sickening. Neither would you want to eat dry, tasteless flour, and I cannot imagine anything more nauseating and tasteless than attempting to eat raw egg whites. However, these three ingredients, as tasteless and unpalatable as they are by themselves, mixed together by the hands of a skillful cook, make angelfood cake.

What's "the Good"?

"All things work together for good"—not for pleasure, comfort, prosperity, health, or joy, but for good.

What is "the good"? It is the good of the *soul* rather than the *body;* the good of the *eternal* rather than the *present.* It is a good sickness that contributes to the health of the soul. It is a kind poverty that increases our eternal riches. It is a welcome loss that becomes eternal gain.

It is with this thought in mind, no doubt, that Paul said in 2 Corinthians 12:5 that he will glory in his infirmities. *Glorying* in his infirmities is more than submitting to them. No one can glory in afflictions because they are afflictions; but if by faith we can see them to be the divinely appointed means whereby we are made more Christlike, we may gladly and humbly glory in them. Paul said that he might have become "puffed up" after his vision of heaven, and so God gave him a "thorn in the flesh" to keep him humble (2 Corinthians 12:7). That thorn in the flesh was painful and hard to bear, but he said, "Most gladly therefore will I rather glory in my infirmities, *that the power of Christ may rest upon me*" (verse 9). It was a good thorn in the flesh, after all, and though Paul prayed three times for God to remove it, each time God's answer was, "My grace is sufficient for thee" (verse 9).

He Has a Purpose

"According to his purpose"—not according to our will, enjoyment, methods, or plans, but His purpose. Then it is plain that the good toward which all things work is the *fulfilling of His purpose*. What is His purpose? Romans 8:29 answers that: "To be conformed to the image of his Son."

What a blessed promise—"all things work together" for one great purpose, that we might daily become *more like our Lord and Savior Jesus Christ.* It takes a variety of experiences to bring that to pass, but when we know His great and eternal purpose, shall we not be submissive clay in the divine Potter's hand? "Whether it be by pleasure or pain, sickness or health, joy or sorrow, life or death, O Lord, that I may only be like the Master—Thy will be done, and Thy purpose accomplished."

The *diamond* must be cut to bring out its beauty, the *gold* must be refined to bring out its purity, the *vine* must be pruned that it may bear more fruit, the *clay* must be molded that it might become a vessel fit for use; and *the child of God* must be cut and refined and pruned and molded that he might become fit for the Master's use. It seems sometimes that the clay will be ruined in the molding, but the purpose of the Potter is the object of the molding; do not flinch, do not resist, but pray.

❖

"Have Thine own way, Lord! Have thine own way!
Thou art the potter, I am the clay.
Mold me and make me after Thy will,
While I am waiting, yielded and still."
—A. A. Pollard

❖

It Costs

We sing, "I would be like Jesus."

Do you really mean it? Do you really want God to have His way in your life? It costs to be like Jesus. Most of us want the *results* without being willing to pay the *price*. You are inviting chastening, correcting, crushing, and remolding when you ask to be Christlike. If you mean it, quit praying for an easy life, with all burdens, hindrances, and disappointments removed, but honestly pray "Have thine *own way.*" Knowing that this is His will for you, submit to Him; whatever He does is "according to his purpose," and His purpose is that you might daily become more like your Savior.

If you learn this secret, you can praise God at all times, in all places, and under any circumstances. Learn this lesson, and you can meet every condition and event in life with a "Praise the Lord" and "God sent it, so it must be good for me." Oh, the joy of knowing we are in God's hands—our lives, our destinies, our possessions, our all! With this surrender to His will there is a calmness and victory that does not depend upon outward surroundings, but is based on the blessed assurance that "all things work together for good." God can mightily use Christians who stay cool in a hot place, sweet in a sour place, big in a crushing place, and little in a big place.

They threw Paul in prison, and out of that dungeon came some of his most precious epistles. I am so glad that Paul did not pray for God to open the jail doors, as he did on another occasion, but I can well imagine that Paul submitted to the will of God with this spirit: "God, you have called me to preach, and I cannot do any preaching in this prison; but if this is where you want me to be, then it is exactly where I want to be." They banished John to Patmos, and from his exile came the Revelation. Had John been like most of us, he no doubt would have complained against God and cried out, "Now why did this have to happen to me? What have I done to deserve such treatment? God send a rescue ship. I do not have time to spend out here alone." But are you not glad that John submitted to the will of God? Much of what we know about the future and our heavenly home we learn from the Revelation. They murdered Stephen, but out of his death came the conviction of Saul of Tarsus. They threw John Bunyan in jail, and out of that jail came *Pilgrim's Progress.*

Are You Willing?

We pray, and then sometimes complain because God answers our prayer. Have you ever prayed, "God, increase my faith?" Then you complained because of the hard chain of events that God sent. How did you expect God to answer that prayer? I know of no way except that He send some hard trial or crushing experience where our faith is taxed to the very limit. Then He gives more faith. Have you ever prayed, "Lord, keep me humble?" Did you expect God to wave a magic wand over you and make you a giant of humility instantly? No, it does not happen that way. God sent some humiliating experience and thus answered your prayer. We pray, "God, draw me nearer," and in answer He sends some sorrow or heartache that drives us to our knees in prayer and to His Word for guidance. We pray, "Make me pure," and He sends the testing, purifying fire. We pray, "Give me patience," and everything seems to go wrong, for "tribulation worketh patience" (Romans 5:3).

Quit praying for an easy life and yield once and for all, right now, to His will, knowing that His eternal purpose is that you might "be conformed to the image of his Son" (Romans 8:29).

Then through faith we can look forward to the time when the work shall be completed, and we "shall be like him; for we shall see him as he is" (1 John 3:2). "As we have borne the image of the earthy [Adam], we shall also bear the image of the heavenly [Christ]." Read 1 Corinthians 15:47–49.

❖

Not till the loom is silent
And the shuttles cease to fly,
Shall God unroll the canvas
And explain the reason why.
The dark threads are as needful
In the weaver's skillful hand,
As the threads of gold and silver
In the pattern He has planned.
—Author unknown

❖

You Can Be Happy

The pursuit of happiness is everyone's inherent

right. But the right in itself does not guarantee the reality. The fact remains that many people have pursued happiness for many years and have never "caught up" with it. Why? God wants us to be happy. He has made abundant provision for our happiness regardless of our circumstances.

Perhaps the problem lies in contentment. To be happy we must be content, satisfied with everything we have and experience in life. That, too, is possible! A careful study of Psalm 37:1–11 will unlock the blessed truth that you can be happy.

Do you have everything your heart desires? No? Why not? God wants you to have it. It is possible. "He shall give thee the desires of thine heart" (Psalm 37:4). There is a simple secret—master it, and you can have everything your heart desires. This is true, but still there has never been a time of more frustration, mental and physical crack-ups, broken homes, crime, and greed than we have today. The root of most of it is discontent—grasping for something beyond reach, striving for something beyond ability, coveting something beyond means, or wishing for something beyond the will of God.

Never have we had so much, and never have we been less satisfied. We see someone else with something better, and we plunge into a mad scramble to get that. It seems that people have become obsessed with the idea that happiness can be secured with "things." God warns, "A man's life consisteth not in the abundance of the things which he possesseth" (Luke 12:15). We are a gadget-conscious generation. We have more "things" than they have had in any other age; yet perhaps we have less real contentment. The more "things" we possess, the more time we have, and consequently more frustration results. Man cannot be happy and content as long as there are unfulfilled desires. For the Christian, it is possible to have everything his heart desires, and with that comes contentment. If you are not content, there is a reason. You either want the wrong things or you want more than God wants you to have. We have developed a false idea of happiness.

What Is Happiness?

I remember a lady in the hospital who was desperately ill. She had been ill a long time and it seemed that progress was slow. She said, "If I could just be well, then I would be the happiest woman in the world." That was her idea of happiness, but there are many healthy people who are not happy. I have known invalids who were perfectly happy and content.

The crippled boy was a bright little fellow in the orthopedic ward of a hospital in Lincoln, Nebraska. He looked wistfully out of the window at the children playing in the street, and said, "If I could just walk, I'd be the happiest boy in the world." But *you* can walk—does that bring *you* happiness?

A woman had undergone surgery on her eyes. The outcome of the operation had not been determined. As the doctor slowly unwound the bandages and suspense mounted, she exclaimed, "If I can just see, I'll be so happy." But is physical sight the foundation for happiness? The man who jumped off the San Francisco Bay Bridge one day could see, but apparently his sight did not bring him contentment.

I talked with a man who had lost his job. His little savings account had vanished and bills were mounting high. His family began to be in want. As he stated his problem, he said, "If I just had a little money . . . just enough to purchase the necessities of life, I'd be happy." But is money the secret of happiness? Many of the richest people are among the most miserable. Perhaps the rich spend more with the psychiatrist than others.

An unemployed man said, "If I just had a job, I'd be happy," but is work the secret of happiness? Most people have a good job, but it has not brought them contentment.

A single girl said to me, "If I just had a husband, I'd be happy." Apparently this is not the secret of happiness. There are thousands of women who do have husbands, but who seem to think that if the judge would grant a release from the marriage it would bring happiness. There are many husbands who would like to be separated from their wives. Does marriage in itself assure happiness?

The general idea seems to be that happiness consists of getting what we do not have. This is the foundation of the problem of discontentment, frustration, and unhappiness—wanting more than we have, whether it be money, possessions, position, health, or achievement.

How Can We Be Happy?

There is only one possible solution, only one way to be happy and content. That is to have everything your heart desires. Let me repeat, it is possible. God says, "He shall bring it to pass" (Psalm 37:5).

You see, the secret is in what you desire—"he shall give thee the desires of thine heart" (Psalm 37:4). Now approach the problem this way:

- First, realize that God the Father loves you and wants the very best for you because you belong to Him. A milk company has "contented cows" because they say contented cows give more and better milk. God wants contented children because contented children produce more and better fruit for His glory.
- Second, remember God deals with the future. We usually think only of the present.

Read it again. It does not say He will give you every "thing" you desire, but He will give you the desires of your heart.

Your foolish heart might desire something that would harm you, and He loves you too much to permit it.

Your selfish heart might desire something that would ruin your life, but His wisdom cannot grant such a request.

Your carnal heart might desire something that would wreck your spiritual life and hinder your growth. His love will not permit it.

Your greedy heart might desire something that would make you a spiritual pauper. His heavenly Father's heart cannot allow it.

Your self-centered heart might desire something that would break your fellowship with Him, and His perfect love cannot grant it.

Your blind heart might desire something for the present that would be a curse to you in the future. He who sees "the end from the beginning" (Isaiah 46:10) must say "No."

When we do not have what we desire, there is something wrong with our desires. We ask for things that would harm us. He promises in Psalm 84:11 that "no good thing" will be withheld. That is true, but still if we are to be content, we must have everything we desire.

Here's the Key!

"He shall give thee the desires of thine heart" (Psalm 37:4). It means that He will put into your heart the desire for the things that He wants you to have. And remember . . . He wants you to have the things that are best for you. When He puts the desire in your heart, you can know that whatever you desire is in His will. Then, and only then, you can have everything you desire. When you ask for it, He who put the desire in your heart loves to grant it. Can you think of any sweeter, higher, better thing? That is perfect contentment—perfect happiness.

But you say, "How can I have Him put the right desires into my heart?" Look at the first part of that verse. "Delight thyself also in the Lord; and he shall give thee the desire of thine heart." It means to find your pleasure in Him. The heart that delights in the Lord finds its truest joy in Him.

If we delight (find our joy) in "things"—possessions, position—the result is frustration and unhappiness. "Delight in Him" means to find your joy in Him. This brings happiness, peace, and contentment.

Delight in His "favour" (Deuteronomy 33:23).

Delight in His "will" (Ephesians 6:6).

Delight in His "service" (Isaiah 41:8).

Delight in His "person" (Psalm 37:4).

Delight in His "presence" (fellowship) (Psalm 16:11).

We should be occupied with Him.

Oh, how few of us "delight in the Lord." Paul expressed it this way, "Christ is all, and in all" (Colossians 3:11).

It's in Him

"Delight thyself also in the Lord; and he shall give thee the desires of thine heart" (Psalm 37:4).

"Christ is all, and in all" (Colossians 3:11). This is the secret of a happy life, the secret of contentment. Then, I am so close to Him that I want only His will for my life. He puts the desire in my heart for the things that are for my good and His glory. Then I can have everything my heart desires. You need proof? It is Psalm 37:23, "The steps of a good man are ordered by the Lord: and *he delighteth in his way*."

"Delight in the Lord."

This is a cure for fretting. "Fret not" (verse 1). To fret is to worry, to fume, to fuss. "Fret not" means "Do not get heated up about it." Why do we fuss and fret? Usually because we want something we do not have and others have. Look at it this way. Spurgeon said, "Who envies the trapped bullock the ribbons and garlands which decorate him as he is led to the slaughter?" That is why God says, "Fret not thyself because of evildoers" (verse 1). Do not fuss because they have more than you do . . . do not envy them. They are like the fat bullock going to the slaughter. The cure for fretting is to be content. How? Delight in the Lord. Do not desire what others have . . . you have *Him*. "Delight thyself in the Lord."

This is the secret of trust (verse 3). "Trust in the Lord." The farmer sows and cultivates, then leaves the harvest to God. What more can he do? He cannot send sunshine and rain. Likewise, we must leave the results to God. I can trust completely in Him if I desire only what He wills. "Delight in the Lord."

This is the result of surrender (verse 5). "Commit thy way unto the Lord; . . . and he shall bring it to pass." "Commit" means to roll your anxiety on Him. Say, "If it is not His will, I do not want it." "Delight in the Lord."

What you want to do and cannot do, what you want to have and cannot have, or what you want to be and cannot be, becomes a burden and leads to frustration and bitterness. Roll it onto Him. Turn your affairs over to God. When I completely surrender myself to Him, then His will becomes my only desire, and so I can have every desire of my heart.

"Delight in the Lord."

This is the foundation of peace (verse 7). "Rest in the Lord." Rest means to "hold still." When we rest in Him we are not fretting, we are not disturbed, we are content.

Dr. Morsey said, "Here is a passenger on a great ocean liner. He lies in the deck chair and rests. The great engines and the mighty propellers drive him across the ocean. When he arrives a friend says, 'How did you get here?' He can honestly answer, 'I rested.' Did he have to struggle? Did he have to fret? Did he have to worry? No. He just rested and trusted the ship to take him across."

Do you have a problem?—Turn it over to Him. Rest in Him. Then when someone asks, "What are you doing about it?" you can say, "I am doing nothing. It is being done for me by One who is perfectly able. I am resting." Anything less than that is not faith. But remember, this is a desire He must put into your heart.

"Delight in the Lord."

This is the basis of exoneration (verse 6): "And he shall bring forth thy righteousness." Sit still and He will clear the slandered. We may be sure that if we look to His honor, He will see to ours. Has someone misunderstood you, abused you, misused your name, and falsely accused you? Delight in your Savior—rest in Him, and "He shall bring forth thy righteousness." There is usually not much use in our seeking to justify ourselves when falsely accused. Someone has said, "Your enemies do not believe your defense, and your friends do not require it." The very effort leads to more anxiety, fretting, and fussing. Simply rest in Him, and "He shall bring forth thy righteousness." Read it this way: "Delight thy *self* in the Lord." After all, it is usually our *self* that has been hurt.

"Delight in the Lord."

This is the cure for anger (verse 8). "Cease from anger, and forsake wrath." The psychologist tells us that anger is a defense mechanism usually based on the fact that we feel insecure in the position we have taken. Perhaps the only way to cease from anger is to delight in Him. Turn your position and your reputation over to Him. We can usually see the "self" in the other person, and this adds to our own discontent. "He has so much 'self' in him, yet he gets along so well . . . Why?" Let's see that we ourselves find our delight in the Lord.

"Delight in the Lord."

This is the key to patience (verse 7). "Wait patiently for him." Waiting is part of resting. Roll the problem on Him. You see, it is God's affair now. Do not fret and fuss. He is able; just wait. His clock is not necessarily synchronized with yours. Because you do not see what He is doing, that does not necessarily mean that He is not working on your behalf. Waiting is proof of faith. Do not turn the thing over to Him and then become impatient and take it out of His hands and try to do it yourself.

Not only wait (we cannot help waiting) but "wait patiently" (verse 7). I have seen many impatient waiters. Because we do not wait patiently, God sometimes has to wait for us. You do not have to wait to begin to delight in Him. You do not have to wait to have every desire fulfilled because "he shall bring it to pass" (verse 5), "He worketh" (1 Corinthians 16:10). It is present tense. He starts when we roll it on to Him. He begins immediately. "Commit," "rest," "trust," "delight"—this is not a life of indolence; it is the greatest incentive to aggressive, earnest, sincere, ambitious Christian living. To know that you shall have every desire of your heart is not only possible, it is His will for you. This is joy. This is delight. This is true Christian victory—to walk so close to Him, to be so yielded to Him, that He can whisper, "This is the way, walk ye in it" (Isaiah 30:21). You can be happy and content because your heart desires only His will for you. He who gave you the desire is able to fulfill it. "Delight thyself also in the Lord; and he shall give thee the desires of thine heart" (Psalm 37:4).

Christian Living

❖

Whatever you think, both in joy and in woe,
Think nothing you would not want Jesus to know.
Whatever you say in a whisper or clear,
Say nothing you would not want Jesus to hear.
Whatever you sing in the midst of your glee,
Sing nothing God's listening ear would displease.
Whatever you write with haste or with heed,
Write nothing you would not want Jesus to read.
Whatever you read, though the page may allure,
Read nothing, unless you are perfectly sure
Consternation would not be seen in your look,
If Christ should say, solemnly, "Show me that book."
Wherever you go, never go where you would fear
God's question being asked you,
"What doest thou here?"

❖

"What? know ye not that your body is the temple of the Holy Ghost which is in you, which ye have of God, and ye are not your own? For ye are bought with a price: therefore glorify God in your body, and in your spirit, which are God's" (1 Corinthians 6:19–20).